My First Facts

My First Body Book

Clive Gifford

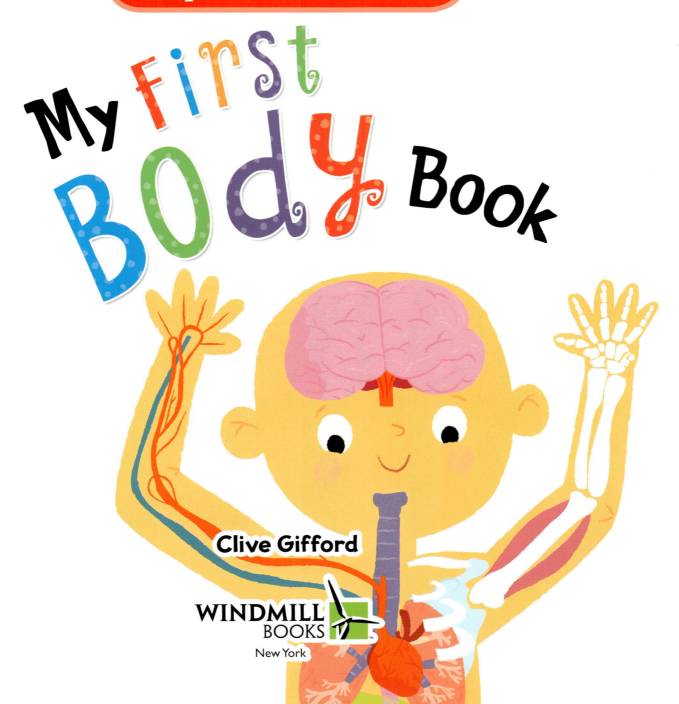

WINDMILL BOOKS
New York

Find out why you sweat on page 8.

Turn to page 41 to discover some activities that will help you feel more calm.

Learn which bit of your brain works out what your eyes are seeing on pages 16–17.

Published in 2023 by **Windmill Books**,
an Imprint of Rosen Publishing,
29 East 21st Street, New York, NY 10010

Copyright © 2018 Miles Kelly Publishing Ltd

All rights reserved. No part of this book may be reproduced in any form without permission in writing from the publisher, except by a reviewer.

Cataloging-in-Publication Data

Names: Gifford, Clive.
Title: My first body book / Clive Gifford.
Description: New York : Windmill Books, 2023. | Series: My first facts
Identifiers: ISBN 9781508198741 (pbk.) | ISBN 9781508198758 (library bound) | ISBN 9781508198765 (ebook)
Subjects: LCSH: Human body--Juvenile literature. | Human physiology--Juvenile literature. | Human anatomy--Juvenile literature.
Classification: LCC QP37.G437 2023 | DDC 612--dc23

Manufactured in the United States of America
CPSIA Compliance Information: Batch CSWM23: For Further Information contact Rosen Publishing, New York, New York at 1-800-237-9932

Find us on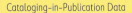

My First Facts

My First BODY Book

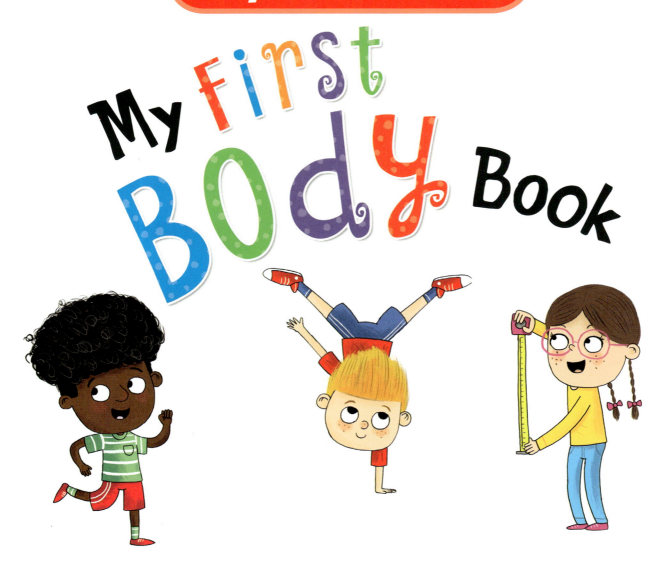

WINDMILL BOOKS
New York

Contents

6 From top to toe

8 Outside in

10 Super skeleton
12 Magic muscles
14 On the move

Strong muscles and bones help me play.

My brain is telling me that my finger hurts!

16 Brainy!
18 On your nerves

20 Super senses
22 Eye-mazing!
24 All ears
26 Smell, taste, and touch

28 Your beating heart
30 Blood takes a trip
32 Breathtaking!
34 Open wide!
36 Food's journey
38 Waste workers
40 Instant messaging
42 Babies!
44 Growing up
46 Feeling better?
48 Test your memory

From top to toe

The human body comes in lots of shapes and sizes. But most bodies are made up of the same parts, which do the same jobs.

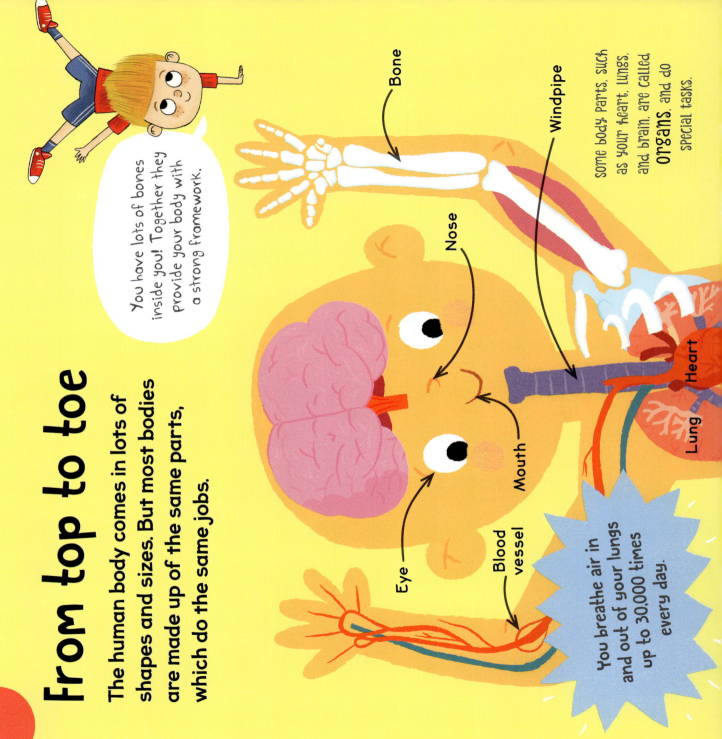

You have lots of bones inside you! Together they provide your body with a strong framework.

Some body parts, such as your heart, lungs, and brain, are called **organs**, and do special tasks.

You breathe air in and out of your lungs up to 30,000 times every day.

Outside in

You're wearing a coat even when you have no clothes on! Your skin is a thin, stretchy, waterproof covering that protects your body.

Outer protection

Skin stops germs from getting into your body. It also has lots of special cells called sensors, which give you your sense of touch.

Sweaty stuff

Your skin releases sweat, which is mostly water. Sweating helps keep you cool. You sweat more from different parts of your body than others.

Your feet can make as much as 17 oz of sweat in one day!

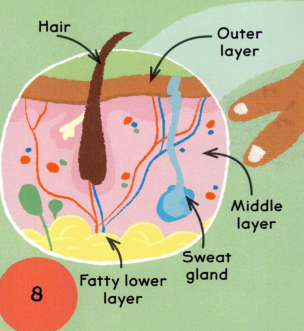

Hair
Outer layer
Middle layer
Sweat gland
Fatty lower layer

Harmful rays from the sun can damage your skin. That's why you should wear sunscreen.

I CAN... MAKE FINGERPRINTS

Press a fingertip onto an ink pad, then onto an uninflated balloon. Wash your fingers and wait a minute for the ink to dry. Blow up the balloon to examine your print. Does it have loops and swirls?

Hairy!

You have around 100,000 hairs on your head. Millions more grow out of your skin elsewhere.

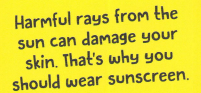

Hair grows out of a tube called a follicle

Hair root

Nailed it

Fingernails give your fingertips protection. They're made from the same materials as hair.

Hairs can be straight, wavy, or curly

Fingernails grow by about 0.5 inch (1.3 cm) every three months.

Super skeleton

Your skeleton is made of more than 200 bones. It supports your body, helps you move, protects extra-special parts such as your brain, and grows as you grow.

Inside a bone
A bone's outside (1) is hard and tough. Inside (2), it looks like honeycomb, with many tiny holes, so it's strong but light. In the middle is the jellylike marrow (3).

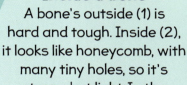

Different types of joints do different jobs. Your knee joint lets you bend and straighten your leg. It is called a hinge joint.

Move it

A joint is where two or more bones meet. There are lots of different types of joints, and they help you to move in different ways.

Phalanges

Tibia

Fibula

Patella

Femur

Pelvis

Your thigh bone (femur) is the longest bone in your body.

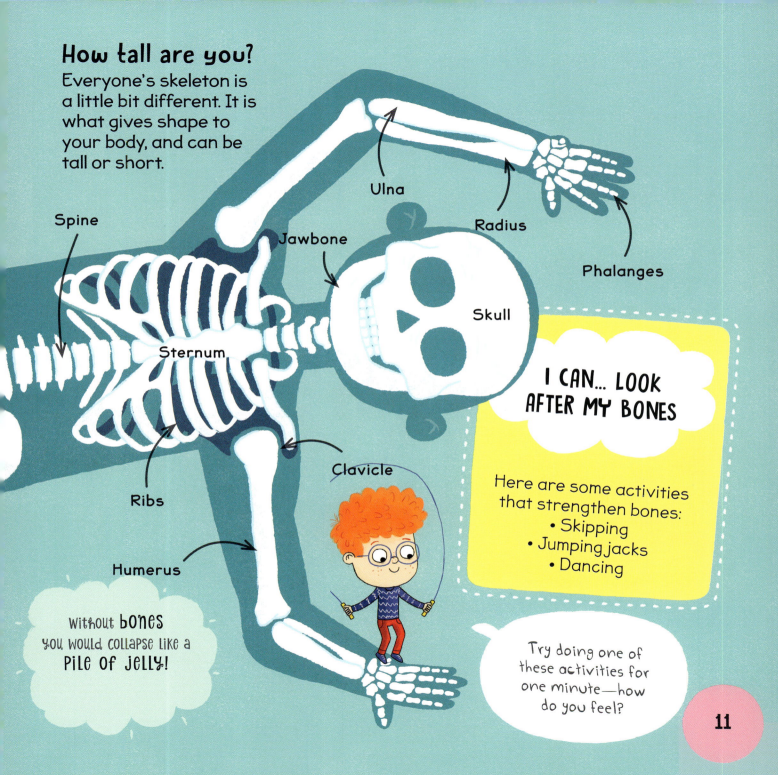

Magic muscles

There are more than 600 muscles in your body. Every move you make, from blinking your eye to lifting a heavy bag, is made by these power-packed parts.

1. Jaw muscles open and close mouth
2. Pectoral muscles move arm and shoulder
3. Deltoid muscles help stretch arm out at the shoulder
4. Biceps muscle bends arm
5. Abdominal muscles help you breathe
6. Thigh muscles straighten your leg

When muscles work, they heat up. If you get too cold, you shiver—your muscles shake a little to help warm you up.

Pulling power

Muscles are made of fibers. Each fiber is made up of long thin cells which are packed together in bundles.

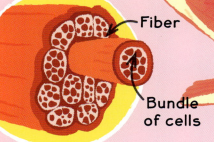

Fiber

Bundle of cells

12

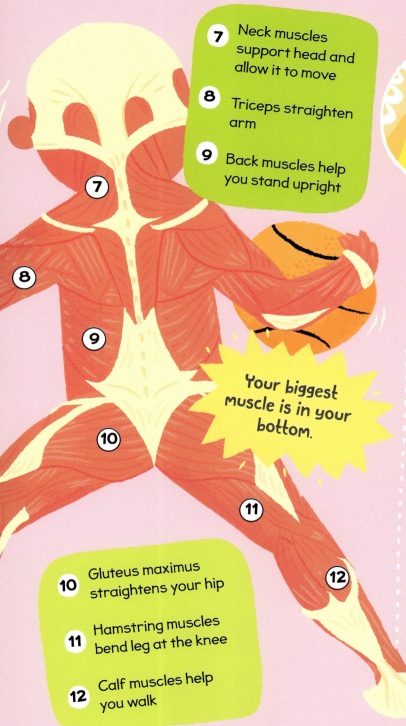

7 Neck muscles support head and allow it to move

8 Triceps straighten arm

9 Back muscles help you stand upright

10 Gluteus maximus straightens your hip

11 Hamstring muscles bend leg at the knee

12 Calf muscles help you walk

Your biggest muscle is in your bottom.

Biceps contracts

Biceps relaxes

To make a muscle pull a part of your body, your brain sends a signal to the muscle for its fibers to **contract** (shorten). When the muscle stops pulling and **relaxes**, it returns to its previous length.

I CAN... FLEX MY MUSCLES

With your arm hanging down at your side, relaxed, place one hand on your biceps muscle. To feel the muscle shortening, bend the arm at the elbow, bringing your hand toward your shoulder.

On the move

Joints are the places where bones meet. Some joints, like the ones between bones in your skull, are fixed in place. Many other joints allow your body to move in different directions.

Your **elbow** is a **hinge joint**, like the hinge on a door. It can open or close to bend or straighten your arm.

Your fingers and toes contain hinge joints, too!

Your **neck** contains a **turning joint**. It allows your head to swivel to the left and right.

Rotate

Your **shoulder** is a **ball-and-socket** joint. It can move in a wide range of directions.

14

A special kind of joint in your foot has bones that slide across each other, which makes your feet very flexible.

I CAN... FEEL MY FINGER JOINTS

Move your fingers and thumbs around. Feel the different places where they bend and move. Can you count the number of joints in the fingers and thumb of one of your hands?

Bone home

The bones of moving joints are held in place by strong and stretchy straps called ligaments. Muscles are joined to bones by strong cords called tendons.

Knee joint

- Femur
- Tendon
- Ligament
- Cartilage is a slippery material that covers the ends of bones in a joint
- Tibia

Cartilage helps joint bones slide smoothly against each other.

15

Brainy!

About the size of a cauliflower, your brain controls all the parts of your body. It is where you store memories and have ideas. Different bits of your brain all do different jobs.

Skull

Brain stem

The brain stem connects your brain to the rest of your body, and controls breathing and swallowing.

The front of your brain is where you plan things and solve problems. (2)

Ouch! Your sense of touch and how you feel pain is handled here. (1)

Sounds are recognized here — it's called the temporal lobe. (3)

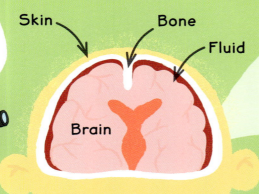

Skin • Bone • Fluid • Brain

"This part works out what your eyes actually see. (5)"

Bonehead
Your skull acts like a bony crash helmet. Inside there's more protection—the brain floats in liquid that cushions it from bumps to your head.

"This part keeps you balanced and all your body's parts working together well. (4)"

Right and left
Your brain has two sides—left and right. Each half controls the opposite side of your body. If you throw a snowball with your left hand, it's the right side of your brain that told it to!

I CAN... TEST MY MEMORY
Look at the eight objects on the tray. Then, close the book and count to 40. Can you remember all of the objects?

Brain cells
Your brain is made up of millions of nerve cells called neurons. These connect to each other as you learn, with as many as 10,000 connections each.

Nerve Cell
Dendrites receive messages
Axon sends messages

On your nerves

Your body is always chatting to your brain about how it is doing. The info travels through the nervous system—a network of nerves that extends all over your body.

Electric!

Nerves are made up of lots of nerve cells. Signals pass through each nerve cell like tiny sparks of electricity.

Nerve signals can travel through your spinal cord at 266 miles (428 km) per hour—faster than a race car!

Signals from other **nerve cells** travel up through these tiny branches

Electrical signal

Brain

Hotline

Your brain is linked to your body by your spinal cord. Your spine (backbone) helps protect it.

Millions of messages travel up and down the spinal cord each day.

Spinal cord

Arm nerves

18

Speedy signals

All parts of your body tell your brain about what is happening and where they are. In return, your brain sends out signals, telling those parts what to do — to move your foot away from something sharp, for example.

Most nerve cells are tiny, but some are almost 3 feet (1 m) long!

1 Nerves sense pain, and send a signal from the foot up the leg and through the spinal cord to the brain

2 Brain sends signal back to the leg, telling it to lift the foot away

I CAN... TEST MY REACTIONS

Hold your thumb and first finger half an inch apart. Get a friend to hold a ruler just above the gap. When they let go, try to grip the ruler. How much of it drops through your fingers? Swap jobs. Are your friend's reactions faster?

19

Super senses

Your body uses its senses to learn about itself and the world. Senses take in information, turn it into electrical signals, and send it to your brain.

Sight
Your eyes give you your sense of sight. Each eye sees a slightly different view. Your brain puts them together to form a clear picture.

Your sense of balance keeps you upright. Spinning around makes this sense work less well, causing you to feel wobbly and dizzy.

Touch
This sense works all over your body and tells you what objects feel like.

Your skin contains lots of cells that can feel warmth or cold.

Taste
Special cells in your mouth and on your tongue let you taste. Without them, a cookie and a carrot would taste the same!

Hearing
You can hear a wide range of sounds. Some are high-pitched, like a whistle. Others are low, like the rumble of a thunderstorm.

Your LIPS and TONGUE are the parts of your body most SENSITIVE to heat.

Smell
Cells inside your nose allow you to recognize thousands of different smells.

Where's MY cookie?

I CAN... USE MY BODY SENSE

Bits of your body tell your brain their position without you looking at them or thinking about them. This sense is called proprioception. To use it, close your eyes and try to touch your nose with your right thumb.

Using "pro-pree-o-sep-shan" is easier than saying it!

21

Eye-mazing!

Your eyes let light in to give you your sense of sight. Light travels through your eye to the retina at the back. There, special cells turn light into electrical signals. The signals travel to your brain, which works out what you are seeing.

Letting in light

Each eye has a pupil—a hole that lets in light. Around this is an iris that contains muscles that change the pupil's size to let in the right amount of light.

Eyelashes

Cornea (see-through covering)

Pupil

Lens focuses the light onto the retina

Iris may be brown, blue, green, or gray

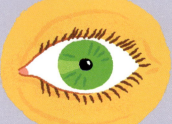

In bright light, the pupil **shrinks** and lets less light in.

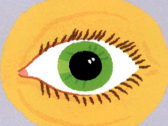

In dim light, the pupil gets **bigger** to let more light in.

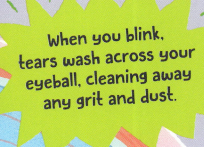

When you blink, tears wash across your eyeball, cleaning away any grit and dust.

A bit of a blur?

Some people's eyeballs are a bit too long or short. This means things either nearby or far away appear blurry. Glasses or contact lenses can usually correct these problems.

Eye tests check if your eyes are healthy and can see well.

Retina

Optic nerve connects eye to brain

Eyeball is full of jelly

I CAN... TRICK MY SIGHT

Optical illusions can trick your eyes and brain. Is the left table longer than the right? It looks like it is, but use a ruler and you'll find they're both the same size!

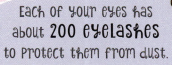

Each of your eyes has about **200 eyelashes** to protect them from dust.

All ears

The big flaps on the side of your head are just the start of what happens when you hear a sound. Your sense of hearing comes from a chain of events that happen mostly inside your head.

Good vibrations

Sounds are vibrations in the air. They can be quiet or loud, high, or low. They are made by people's voices, machines, and many other things.

Sound travels through air at over **620 miles** (998 km) per hour—faster than many **jet planes!**

Bone of skull

Ear canal

Eardrum

1 The outer ear gathers in sounds like a funnel.

Sticky ear wax coats the ear canal. It protects your ear from dirt, dust, and small insects.

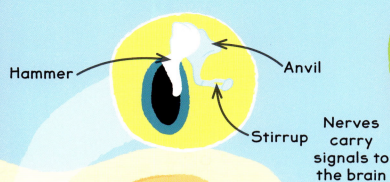

Hammer — Anvil — Stirrup

Nerves carry signals to the brain

3 The ossicles are the three smallest bones in your body. They take vibrations from the eardrum and pass them to the cochlea.

4 The cochlea is a space filled with liquid and many tiny hairs. Sounds make the liquid ripple. The hairs feel the ripples and turn them into electrical signals.

2 When sounds reach the eardrum (a thin piece of special skin), they make it vibrate back and forth.

Are your guesses better using two ears or one?

I CAN... TEST MY HEARING

Close your eyes, place a hand tight over one ear, and ask a friend to make sounds from different parts of the room. Can you guess which direction the sound comes from? Try again, this time with both ears uncovered.

Smell, taste, and touch

These three senses help you enjoy food and drinks. They also warn you of dangers such as sharp objects or food that may make you sick.

Smelly stuff

Invisible smell particles float in the air and are breathed in. Tiny cells high up in your nose detect these particles and send electrical signals to the brain.

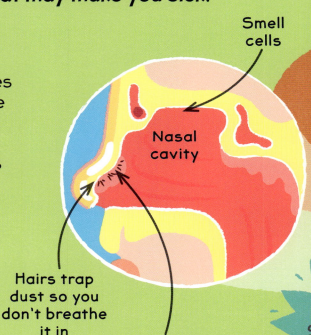

Smell cells

Nasal cavity

Hairs trap dust so you don't breathe it in

Mucus (slimy liquid) in the nostrils traps dirt and germs

This smells bad! Eating it might make me sick.

You sneeze to get rid of things like dust, which your body doesn't like.

Taste sensation

Your tongue's surface, as well as the roof and sides of your mouth, contain little clumps of cells called taste buds. These detect flavors and send signals to your brain.

There are between 2,000 and 8,000 taste buds on your tongue.

Nostril

Taste buds on tongue

I CAN... TRY DIFFERENT TASTES

Your taste buds recognize five major flavors. The more foods you try, the more your brain learns. When you try a new food, think about which flavors you can taste.

Bitter

Umami (savory)

Sweet

Sour

Salty

Magic touch

Your skin is packed with special touch sensors that feel things. Your sense of touch can help you tell if something is rough, smooth, sharp, sticky, wet, or dry.

Your fingertips and lips have more **touch sensors** than anywhere else on your body.

27

Your beating heart

Your heart is an organ made mostly of muscle. It is one of the most powerful muscles, pumping blood all around the body.

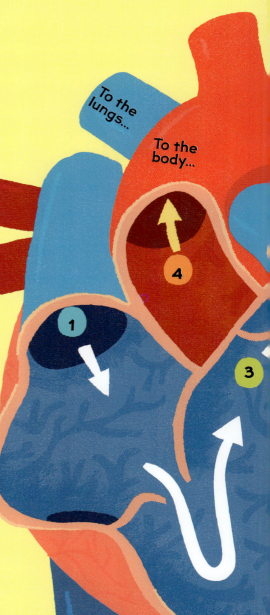

To the lungs...

To the body...

1 Blood low in oxygen enters the right side of your heart.

Your heart is about the same size as your clenched fist.

2 Your heart pumps the low-oxygen blood to your lungs.

In a year, your heart PUMPS enough blood to fill an Olympic swimming pool!

Power pump
Your heart is tireless—it beats (pumps) around 100,000 times per day. That's nearly 70 times every minute.

To the lungs...

2

4 The heart pumps the oxygen-rich blood out to the rest of the body.

I CAN... FEEL MY PULSE

You can feel your heartbeat at places on your body called pulse points. Lightly place two fingertips on the inside of your wrist. How fast is your heart beating?

3 After it has collected oxygen from the lungs, the blood travels back to the left side of the heart.

Pacemakers
Special cells send out signals to make your heart beat at the right speed. If these signals aren't working, a doctor may fit a device called a pacemaker to correct it.

Oxygen is a gas we breathe in. Every bit of your body needs oxygen to work. Oxygen is carried in your blood by red blood cells.

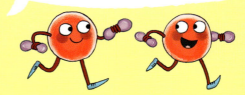

Blood takes a trip

Blood transports useful things around your body such as oxygen and nutrients from food. It's pumped by the strong muscle of your heart.

Quick trip
Your blood completes its journey around your body in under one minute. It travels through tubes called vessels.

2 Then it flows into smaller vessels called capillaries.

1 Blood is pumped out of the heart in big vessels called arteries.

Heart

3 Once it has delivered everything, blood travels back to the heart in vessels called veins.

A drop of blood one millimeter across can contain 5 million red blood cells!

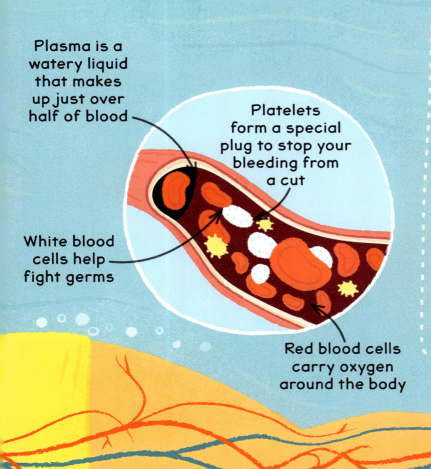

Plasma is a watery liquid that makes up just over half of blood

Platelets form a special plug to stop your bleeding from a cut

White blood cells help fight germs

Red blood cells carry oxygen around the body

I CAN... MAKE MY BLOOD MOVE FASTER

Take your pulse, then take it again after doing 20 jumping jacks. It will be quicker the second time, because your heart is moving your blood faster to supply your body with more oxygen and energy.

If all your blood vessels were laid end to end, they would go around the world two and a half times!

31

Breathtaking!

Oxygen is a gas that makes up about one fifth of air. Your body needs lots of oxygen to turn food into energy. You gain oxygen by breathing air into your lungs.

I CAN... MEASURE MY BREATHING

Count how many times you breathe in and out in a minute. Run on the spot for 30 seconds, then count again. How many more breaths did you take after being active?

When resting, most people take 12 to 20 breaths per minute.

2 Air is sucked into your mouth and nose. It travels down your windpipe, which branches left and right—one branch to each lung.

Nose

Mouth

Windpipe

An average person breathes in more than **2,000 gallons** (7,570 L) of air a day.

32

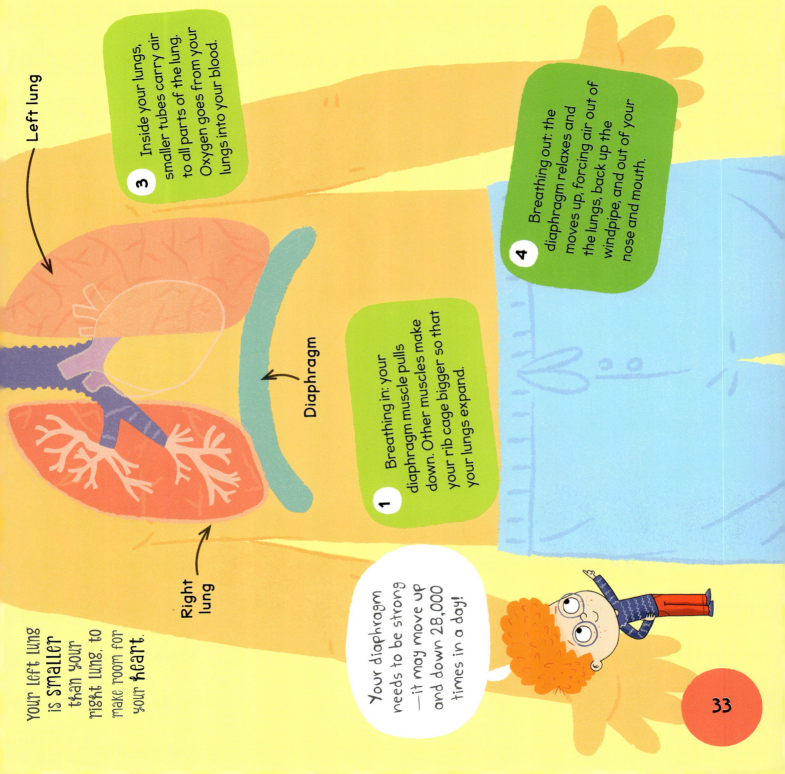

Open wide!

Your mouth helps you speak, taste, and breathe. It is also packed full of teeth which cut, crush, grind, and chew your food as you eat.

Growing up

You'll have two sets of teeth in your life. Your 20 baby teeth start falling out when you're about six years old, and are replaced by a set of 32 adult teeth.

The four canine teeth are more cone-shaped to rip and tear food

- Tonsil
- Uvula
- Gums
- Tongue

The eight incisor teeth cut and chop food when you bite

- Enamel
- Dentine
- Blood vessels
- Nerves
- Root holds tooth in place

A tooth's root can be twice as long as the rest of the tooth.

Mouthwatering

The liquid in your mouth is called saliva. It helps dissolve some parts of food and wets the rest, making it easier for you to chew.

I CAN... BRUSH MY TEETH BRILLIANTLY

Always brush your teeth in the morning and before you go to bed. Brush both the back and front of every tooth up and down. It should take 2–3 minutes. Rinse your toothbrush when you're done.

The protective outer layer of your teeth is called enamel, and it's the hardest substance in your whole body.

Molar and premolar teeth grind and chew food so that you can swallow it

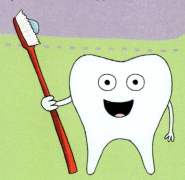

Look how shiny I am!

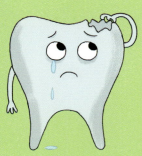

Toothache!

The pain of toothache may be caused by the enamel of your teeth being damaged by decay. This can happen if you eat lots of sugary foods and don't brush your teeth well and often.

Food's journey

You need food for energy, to stay healthy, and for your body to grow and repair itself. When you eat, your food starts a journey through your digestive system.

When empty, your stomach is the size of a tennis ball, but when full it can stretch to almost the size of a soccer ball!

I CAN... EAT WELL

Eating healthily gives your body the energy and all the other things it needs to grow and look after itself. Try to eat several colorful fresh fruits and vegetables as part of every meal.

Chewing breaks up food into tiny pieces.

Mouth

Tongue and throat muscles help you swallow

Food travels down this long tube and into your stomach

Stomach

Large intestine

Small intestine

Appendix

Your small intestine is far from small... it measures 19-22 feet (5.8-6.7 m) long—at least four times as tall as you!

In your tummy
Your stomach is a stretchy bag that can expand to hold a big meal. Food is churned around inside it for hours. Strong chemicals turn it into a gloopy soup.

Food tube
In the small intestine, food is broken down more. Useful bits go into your blood, to be sent around your body. The rest travels into the large intestine.

Turn the page to see what happens in the large intestine.

waste workers

Lots is left behind after all the goodness from your food has traveled into your blood. This waste material sets off on its own journey.

Recycler
The large intestine is about 5 feet (1.5 m) long. It absorbs water and any last useful bits from food. Any leftover waste leaves your body when you go to the bathroom.

Tiny helpers
Millions of bacteria (tiny creatures) live in your large intestine. Many help your body absorb goodness from food. They also create gas, which leaves you via your bottom.

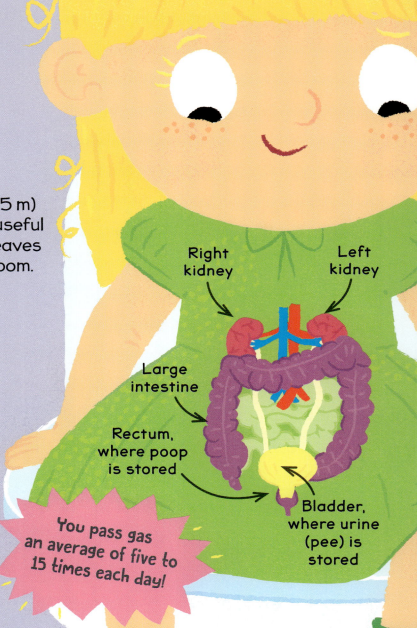

Right kidney

Left kidney

Large intestine

Rectum, where poop is stored

Bladder, where urine (pee) is stored

You pass gas an average of five to 15 times each day!

Your poop is about three-quarters water. The rest is solid waste. Almost one-third of the solid stuff in poop is made up of dead bacteria!

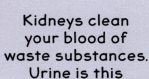

Each kidney gets rid of 35-52 ounces (1-1.5 L) of urine a day!

Kidneys clean your blood of waste substances. Urine is this waste, along with some water.

I CAN... WASH MY HANDS

It's important to wash your hands thoroughly with soap and warm water after you've been to the toilet. This will make sure your hands are free of germs. It should take the same amount of time as singing the "Happy Birthday" song twice.

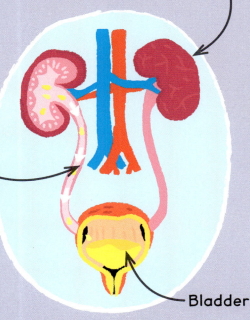

Ureters are tubes that carry urine from the kidneys to the bladder

Bladder

"Happy birthday to you, happy birthday to you..."

Time to go

Most people's bladders can hold around 10 ounces (0.3 L) of urine. When your bladder is full, it sends signals to your brain that it's time to go to the toilet.

Instant messaging

Chemicals called hormones travel around your body, telling different parts what to do and not to do. They're very bossy!

Growth hormone is made in the pituitary gland. It helps you grow big and strong.

Small but mighty

Your pea-sized pituitary gland is inside your head, just behind your nose. It makes lots of different hormones.

Most hormones travel through **blood** to reach the parts they want to command.

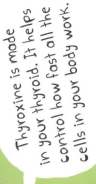

Thyroxine is made in your thyroid. It helps control how fast all the cells in your body work.

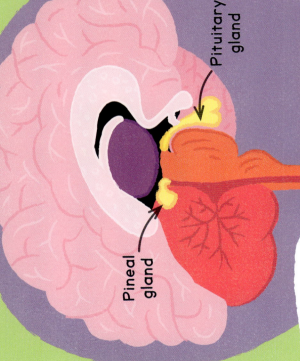

Pituitary gland

Pineal gland

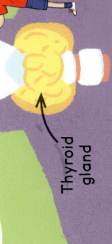

Thyroid gland

Helping glands

Hormones are made by little organs in your body called glands. They make more than 40 different hormones.

Melatonin is made in the pineal gland. It tells your body when to feel sleepy or wide awake.

I CAN... FEEL CALM

It's normal to be a bit scared, sad, or angry sometimes. Always talk to a grown-up if something is worrying you. Here are some extra things you can do to feel better:
- Take three slow, deep breaths
- Listen to favorite music
- Stroke a pet

Diabetes is an illness that affects people whose bodies can't make enough insulin.

Thymus

Adrenal glands

Pancreas

Left kidney

Right kidney

Thymosin is made in your thymus gland. It helps your body make more special white blood cells to fight infections.

The adrenal glands release adrenaline when you are scared. It gives you extra energy so that you can face danger, or run.

Insulin is made in the pancreas. It travels in your blood, helping to control the amount of sugar in your body.

41

Babies!

Everyone starts out as a single tiny egg—smaller than a period on this page. Lots of growth and amazing changes take place before you are born.

Beginning
A cell from a man and a cell from a woman join together inside the woman.

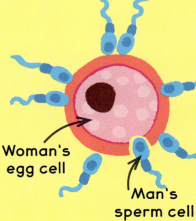
Woman's egg cell
Man's sperm cell

Dividing
The new cell splits into two cells, then four cells. It keeps on dividing into more and more cells. After three weeks, the ball of cells is 2–3 millimeters long.

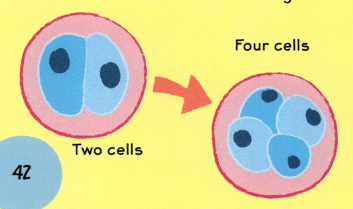
Two cells
Four cells

Growing fast
After nine weeks, the group of cells is the size of a grape. By 14 weeks, the group of cells (now called a fetus) is the size of a lemon. By 30 weeks, it can weigh as much as a coconut.

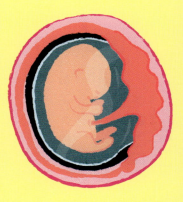

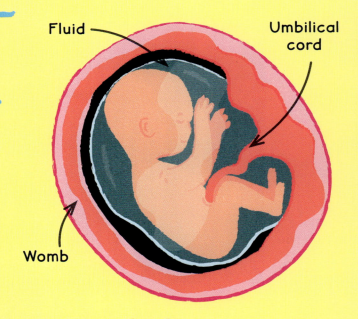
Fluid
Umbilical cord
Womb

Fed and protected
The fetus floats in fluid, which protects it from bumps. The mom supplies it with oxygen and food from her blood, through a tube called the umbilical cord.

I CAN... LEARN ABOUT BABY ANIMALS

One of these animals spends 645 days inside its mom before it is ready to be born. The other is ready in just 33 days. But which is which?

Answer:
Rabbit: 33 days
Asian elephant: 645 days

Ready, steady...

After almost 9 months inside mom's body, most babies are big enough to be born.

Every 10 seconds, more than 40 babies are born around the world!

Baby is curled up tightly

Mom's backbone

The umbilical cord is removed when you are born. What's left behind becomes your belly button.

...Go!

Muscles push the baby down and out of the womb and eventually the baby is born.

Growing up

Being born is just the start! You keep growing for many years from a small baby into an adult. But even then your body will still keep changing as you get older and older.

Your brain doubles in weight by the age of two!

I CAN... LEARN THINGS

You are growing and changing all the time. Can you think of one thing that you can do now that you couldn't do last year?

From **birth**, you grow fast. By the time you are one year old, you may be 9 inches (23 cm) taller than when you were born.

A **two-year**-old has learned how to walk and is learning about the world around them.

From **four** to **ten** years old, most children grow around 2.4 inches (6 cm) taller each year.

I can write my name.

TEENAGE girls grow breasts and their hips get wider.

A baby's head is one-quarter of his or her total height. An adult's is only one-eighth.

Child to adult
The time during which children start to become adults is called puberty. Many changes take place during these years.

ADULT men and women are fully grown. They may choose to have a baby themselves, starting the whole growing-up process again!

TEENAGE boys' voices get deeper and they grow hair on their faces.

Humans stop getting taller around the age of 20. But our ears keep on growing slowly for the rest of our lives!

During puberty, you may grow more than 4.5 inches (11.4 cm) in a single year!

Feeling better?

Your amazing body protects you against illness and disease every day. It is also great at repairing itself. Sometimes, though, it needs a little help from doctors and nurses.

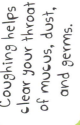

"Coughing helps clear your throat of mucus, dust, and germs."

Inside your body, some **white blood cells** fight diseases by swallowing up germs.

Too hot!

A fever is when your body temperature is a lot higher than normal. An adult may use a thermometer to check how hot you are.

More than 200 different viruses can cause you to catch a cold.

Scabby stuff

Blood thickens around a cut on your skin. It then hardens to form a scab, which stops germs from getting into your body.

Broken bones

Bones are strong but can be broken by an accident such as a fall. Children's bones heal quicker than adults'.

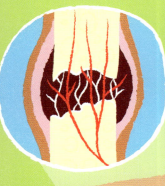

1 Doctors take X-ray photos that let them see inside your body.

2 Plaster cast holds a broken bone in the correct position so that it can heal.

3 Lots of new cells and blood vessels grow where the break occurs. Over time, these repair the bone.

Broken bones

Vaccines helped wipe out a nasty disease called smallpox.

I CAN... GET A GOOD NIGHT'S SLEEP

Sleep is a time for your body to rest and repair, to get ready for the next day. Make sure your bed is comfy and not full of toys. Try to sleep in the dark and don't play computer games just before you head to bed.

Extra help

A vaccine is made from a weak or harmless version of a disease. It causes your body to build up its defenses against the real disease.

Test your memory

Now it's time to find out what you've learned. The information to answer these questions can be found on the pages of this book.

How much can you remember about your body?

1. What is the name for the jellylike substance inside your bones?
2. Where is your biggest muscle?
3. What kind of joint is your shoulder joint?
4. Which part of your body controls all the other parts?
5. What does your spine help to protect?
6. What is the name of the hole in your eye that lets in light?
7. Where are the smallest bones in your body?
8. Which type of blood cell helps fight germs?
9. Where is urine (pee) stored before it leaves your body?
10. When will your ears stop growing?

Check your answers here!

ANSWERS
1. Marrow
2. In your bottom
3. A ball-and-socket joint
4. Your brain
5. Your spinal cord
6. The pupil
7. In your ear
8. White blood cells
9. In your bladder
10. They won't—they will keep growing for your whole life